Looking After Our Minds

By Vikki McIntyre

Illustrated by Mila Aydingoz

We respect and honour Aboriginal and Torres Strait Islander Elders past, present and future. We acknowledge the stories, traditions and living cultures of Aboriginal and Torres Strait Islander peoples on this land and commit to building a brighter future together.

Library For All Ltd.

Let's yarn about mental health

Sadness

DEPRESSION

TRAUMA

Anxiety

Sometimes, we carry things inside that no one else can see. Sadness, worry, bad memories, or heavy thoughts can make us feel like we're walking around with a big stone in our chest.

These feelings have names — like depression, trauma, anxiety, or just deep sadness. They don't mean we're weak. They mean we're human.

Our mob have been through a lot — past and present. Our families, our communities, and our spirits have carried stories of strength, but also of hurt.

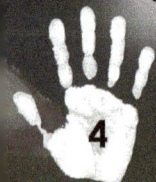

When hard things happen, they can leave marks inside us. That's why it's important to look after our mental health, just like we look after our bodies.

What is mental health?

Our mental health affects how we think, feel, and cope with life. Good mental health helps us enjoy life, learn, make friends, and deal with stress. But sometimes things go wrong, and our mental health can suffer.

Understanding our feelings

Sadness: Everyone feels sad sometimes. But if the sadness doesn't go away or keeps coming back, it might be time to talk about it.

Anxiety: When worry takes over, it can make our heart race, our tummy hurt, or make us feel like something bad is going to happen. It can be hard to sleep or concentrate when we feel anxious.

Depression: This is more than just feeling sad. Depression can make us feel numb, tired, or hopeless for a long time. We might stop enjoying things or want to stay away from people.

Trauma: Trauma can happen when we live through something scary or painful — like losing someone, being hurt, or seeing violence. These things can stick with us and show up in our dreams, thoughts, or bodies.

Signs someone might need help

Not wanting to eat or eating too much

Getting angry or upset easily

Not wanting to be around friends or family

Having trouble sleeping and feeling tired all the time, even after sleeping

Saying things like "I'm no good," or "I wish I wasn't here."

If you or someone you know feels this way, **it's okay to speak up**. Telling someone can be the first step to feeling better.

Mob ways to look after your mental health

Yarning: Talking with someone you trust — an Elder, aunty, uncle, friend, or teacher — can lighten the load. A good yarn can heal.

Country: Being on Country helps us feel calm and strong. Listening to the birds, walking barefoot, or sitting by the fire reminds us we belong.

Culture: Dance, song, art, language, and ceremony connect us to our ancestors. They help us feel proud and remind us of who we are.

Movement: Playing sport, walking, or dancing can help your body and brain feel better.

There are many ways to care for your spirit and mind. Some come from culture and Country. Others come from health clinics and counsellors. Both ways can work together.

Western ways

Talking to a counsellor: These are people trained to listen and help. They can teach you ways to manage big feelings.

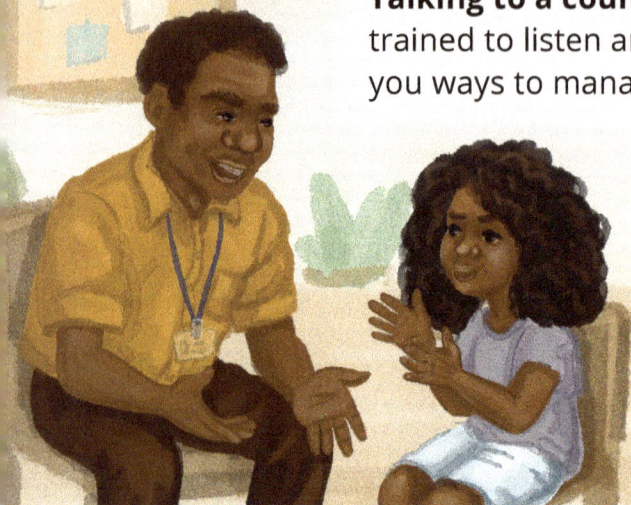

Seeing a doctor: Sometimes doctors can help with medicine or treatment that supports your mental health.

Writing or drawing: Some people find it helps to write in a journal or draw their feelings.

Breathing exercises: Slowing your breathing can calm your body and mind. Try breathing in for 4 seconds, holding for 4, and breathing out for 4.

You are not alone

You are never alone in how you feel. Many people, including kids and teenagers, struggle with their mental health sometimes. You are strong for recognising your feelings. You are even stronger when you ask for help.

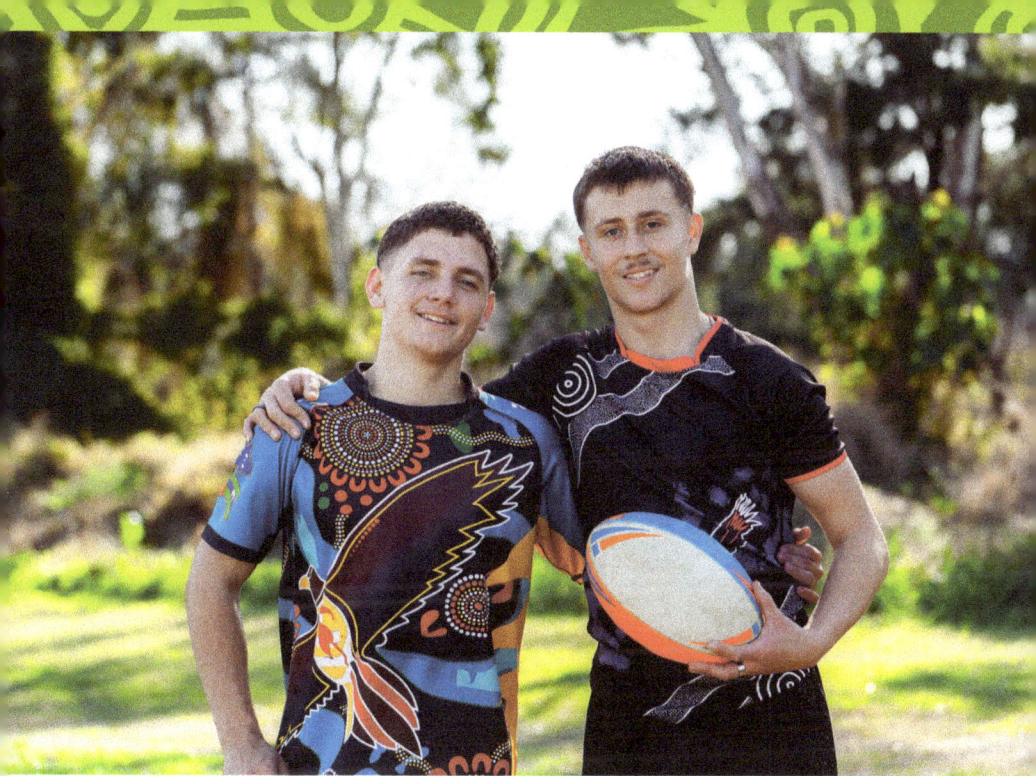

You deserve care. You deserve to feel safe and heard. There is always someone who will listen.

**Don't be shame to feel sad or anxious.
Don't be shame to talk to someone.
Healing is our right.**

Final words

Sadness
DEPRESSION
Anxiety
TRAUMA

Looking after your mental health is like looking after Country. It needs care, connection, and time. Some days will be hard. But remember, you carry the strength of your mob, your culture, and your story. You are important. Your feelings matter. There are people — both from your community and in clinics — who want to help you feel strong again.

Keep talking. Keep walking. Keep healing.

Stay deadly!

Getting help

If you need to talk to someone now, here are some places that can help.

13YARN: 13 92 76 or visit www.13yarn.org.au

A free and confidential support line run by mob, for mob 24/7.

Kids Helpline: 1800 55 1800 or visit www.kidshelpline.com.au

For anyone aged 5 to 25. Talk to someone about anything, anytime.

Headspace: 1800 650 890 or visit www.headspace.org.au

Mental health support for young people. You can find local centres or chat online.

Beyond Blue: 1300 22 4636 or visit www.beyondblue.org.au

Information and support to help everyone in Australia look after their mental health.

Photo Credits

You can use these questions to talk about this book with your family, friends and teachers.

What did you learn from this book?

Describe this book in one word. Funny? Scary? Colourful? Interesting?

How did this book make you feel when you finished reading it?

What was your favourite part of this book?

About the author

Vikki McIntyre was born in Sydney and grew up in the western suburbs. Her ancestral Country is the south coast of New South Wales. She descends from the saltwater people of the Dharawal language group. Vikki is happiest when she can feel sand under her feet and smell saltwater in the air.

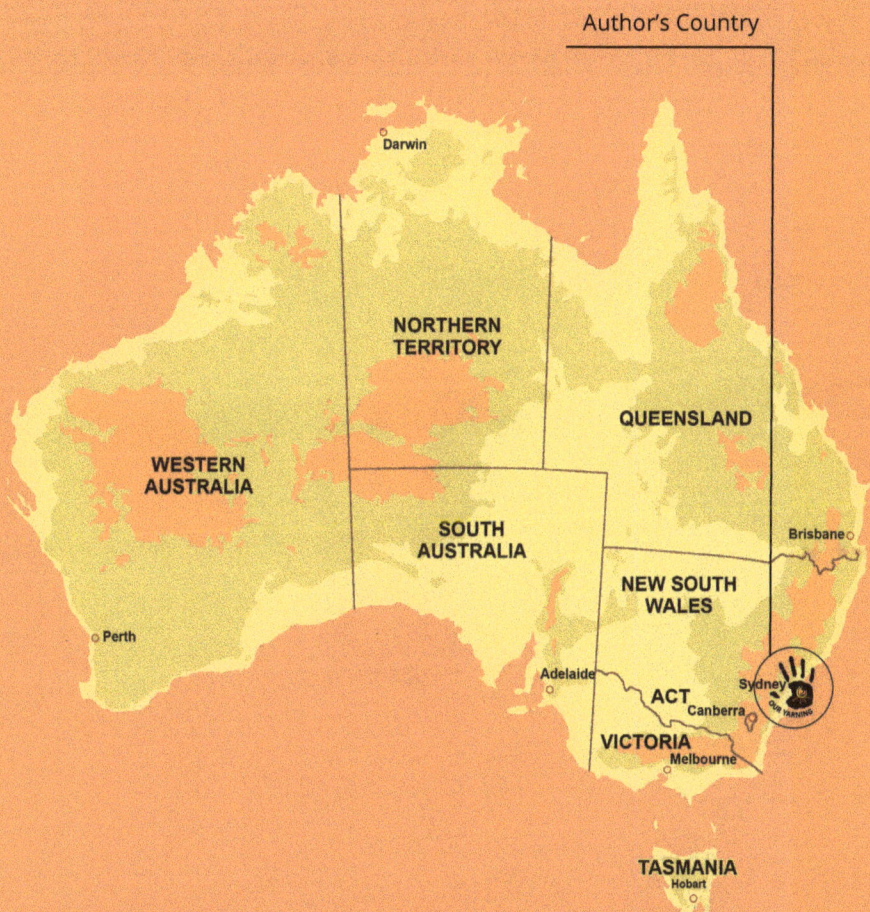

Author's Country

Darwin

NORTHERN
TERRITORY

QUEENSLAND

WESTERN
AUSTRALIA

SOUTH
AUSTRALIA

Brisbane

NEW SOUTH
WALES

Perth

Adelaide

Sydney

ACT
Canberra

VICTORIA
Melbourne

TASMANIA
Hobart

Our Yarning

The Our Yarning collection aligns with the Australian Curriculum through the Cross-Curriculum Priorities — Aboriginal and Torres Strait Islander Histories and Cultures. The collection provides an authentic opportunity for learning and embedding Aboriginal and Torres Strait Islander perspectives because it is written by Aboriginal and Torres Strait Islander people.

We know that children learn better, and enjoy reading more, when they see themselves in the stories, characters and illustrations of the books they read.

To download the app, visit the Google Play Store or Apple Store and search 'Our Yarning'.

libraryforall.org

You're reading Upper Primary

Learner – Beginner readers

Start your reading journey with short words, big ideas and plenty of pictures.

Level 1 – Rising readers

Raise your reading level with more words, simple sentences and exciting images.

Level 2 – Eager readers

Enjoy your reading time with familiar words, but complex sentences.

Level 3 – Progressing readers

Develop your reading skills with creative stories and some challenging vocabulary.

Level 4 – Fluent readers

Step up your reading skills with playful narratives, new words and fun facts.

Middle Primary – Curious readers

Discover your world through science and stories.

Upper Primary – Adventurous readers

Explore your world through science and stories.

Looking After Our Minds

First published 2025

Published by Library For All Ltd
Email: info@libraryforall.org
URL: libraryforall.org

This book was made possible by the generous contributions of GSK.

gsk

Our Yarning logo design by Jason Lee, Bidjipidji Art

Original illustrations by Mila Aydingoz

Looking After Our Minds
McIntyre, Vikki
ISBN: 978-1-923594-11-1
SKU04965

www.ingramcontent.com/pod-product-compliance
Lightning Source LLC
Chambersburg PA
CBHW042342040426
42448CB00019B/3375